# The Big Quiz

By Sally Cowan

"Get set, kids!" said Tam.

"It is The Big Quiz!"

A top hat can fit in it.
It has not got a zip.
It has a lid ...

You can mix in it.
It can get hot.
But it is not a pan ...

A fox can get in it.
It can nap in it.

# CHECKING FOR MEANING

1. What was the answer to the first quiz question? *(Literal)*

2. How many questions did Kim and Zac answer correctly? *(Literal)*

3. Why did Tam say *Top job, Zac!*? *(Inferential)*

# EXTENDING VOCABULARY

| | |
|---|---|
| **quiz** | What is a *quiz*? What do you need to do to win a *quiz*? |
| **zip** | What are two different meanings of this word? Can you use each one in a sentence to show its meaning? |
| **box** | What are the sounds in this word? Which other words in the text have the *x* sound in them? Is this sound at the start or at the end of the words? |

# MOVING BEYOND THE TEXT

1. Have you ever been in or seen a real quiz? How many players were there?

2. Where can you see a quiz being played?

3. What other types of competitions do you know? Have you been in any of these competitions?

4. How would you feel if you won an important quiz or competition? Why?

## SPEED SOUNDS

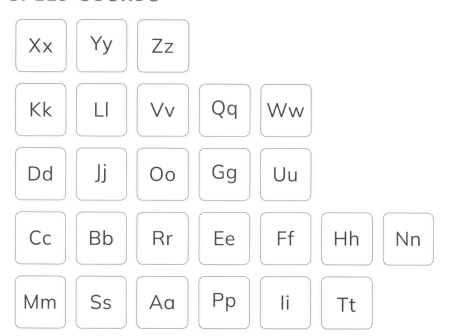

| Xx | Yy | Zz | | | | |
|----|----|----|----|----|----|----|
| Kk | Ll | Vv | Qq | Ww | | |
| Dd | Jj | Oo | Gg | Uu | | |
| Cc | Bb | Rr | Ee | Ff | Hh | Nn |
| Mm | Ss | Aa | Pp | Ii | Tt | |

# PRACTICE WORDS

zip

Quiz

box

Zac

Yes

mix

fox